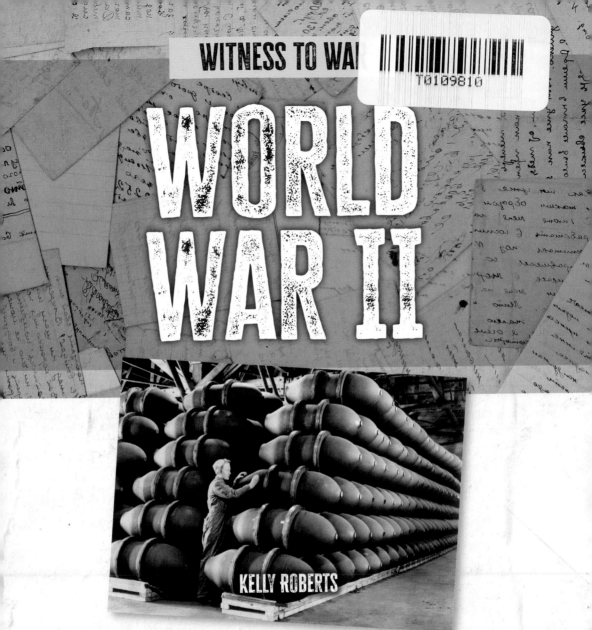

WITNESS TO WAR

WORLD WAR II

KELLY ROBERTS

What can we learn from the people who witnessed war?

CHERITON
CHILDREN'S BOOKS

Published in 2025 by **Cheriton Children's Books**
1 Bank Drive West, Shrewsbury, Shropshire, SY3 9DJ, UK

Copyright 2025 Cheriton Children's Books

First Edition

Author: Kelly Roberts
Designer: Paul Myerscough
Editor: Sarah Eason
Proofreader: Katie Dicker

Picture credits: Cover: U.S. Air Force; Inside: p1: Shutterstock/Everett Collection, p3: German Federal Archive, p4: Shutterstock/Everett Collection, p5: Imperial War Museums, p7: Shutterstock/ Everett Collection, p8: Shutterstock/Everett Collection, p9b: Shutterstock/Everett Collection, p9t: Shutterstock/Everett Collection, p10: Shutterstock/Everett Collection, p11b: Shutterstock/Everett Collection, p11t: Imperial War Museums, p12b: Wikimedia Commons/Imperial Japanese Navy, p12t: Wikimedia Commons/German Air Force, p13: Shutterstock/Alexander Oganezov, p14b: National Archives, p14t: Shutterstock/Everett Collection, p15: National Archives and Records Administration, p16: Imperial War Museums, p17b: National Archives and Records Administration/Dorothea Lange, p17t: Wikimedia Commons/Australian War Memorial, p18: Shutterstock/Everett Collection, p19b: Wikimedia Commons/Dennis Nilsson, p19t: National Archives and Records Administration, p20: Shutterstock/Everett Collection, p21: Library of Congress/Horton (Capt), p22: Imperial War Museums, p23b: Shutterstock/Everett Collection, p23t: National Archives and Records Administration/Stroop: Report, p24: Shutterstock/Everett Collection, p25: Shutterstock/Everett Collection, p26: Shutterstock/ Everett Collection, p27: Shutterstock/Everett Collection, p28: Shutterstock/Everett Collection, p29: U.S. Air Force, p30: Shutterstock/Everett Collection, p31b: Shutterstock/Everett Collection, p31t: Library of Congress/Winsor McCay, p32: Shutterstock, p33b: Shutterstock/Everett Collection, p33t: Shutterstock/Everett Collection, p34b: U.S. Government Printing Office, p34t: Wikimedia Commons, p35b: Shutterstock/Everett Collection, p35t: Imperial War Museums/No 5 Army Film & Photographic Unit, Palmer (Sgt), p36: Shutterstock/Everett Collection, p37: Shutterstock/Everett Collection, p38: German Federal Archive, p39: Shutterstock/Everett Collection, p40: Shutterstock/Everett Collection, p41: United States Department of Energy/Charles Levy, p42: Shutterstock/Rob Crandall, p43: Shutterstock/Everett Collection.

All rights reserved. No part of this book may be reproduced in any form without permission of the publisher, except by a reviewer.

Printed in China

Please visit our website,
www.cheritonchildrensbooks.com
to see more of our high-quality books.

CONTENTS

Chapter 1 World War II.................................4

Chapter 2 A Worldwide War 8

Chapter 3 Families on the Front Line 16

Chapter 4 Women and the War.......................24

Chapter 5 Funding the War 30

Chapter 6 Wiping Out People 36

Chapter 7 The War Comes to an End...................40

A Timeline for War 44

Glossary 46

Find Out More 47

Index and About the Author...................48

CHAPTER 1

WORLD WAR II

When World War I ended in November 1918, people around the world hoped that the terrible bloodshed of that conflict would never be repeated. However, 20 years later, the children of those who had fought in World War I, or worked in the arms factories and hospitals, were again plunged into a horrifying war. They would witness the devastation of war—and in doing so, become a witness to history. In this book we will look at some of their stories and their words as witnesses to war.

Adolf Hitler was the leader of Germany, a country that had suffered great hardship after World War I. Hitler promised to make Germany great again.

WITNESSES TO WAR

In this book we will hear the words of witnesses to the war: the people who experienced the conflict firsthand. We'll discover what impact the war had on them and what we can learn from their accounts. In each case, read the source and the notes, then try to answer the questions.

Hitler Invades

World War II began in September 1939 when Germany, led by Adolf Hitler, invaded Poland. Britain and France then declared war on Germany. By the summer of 1940, Hitler's armies controlled much of Europe, including France. At first, Britain and its **allies** such as France, Australia, South Africa, and New Zealand stood against Germany. They were later joined by other countries. Germany agreed a pact with its main allies, Italy and Japan, in September 1940. After initially forming a pact with the **Soviet Union**, Germany invaded the country in June 1941 and they became enemies, too.

Forced to Act

Japan had invaded China in 1937. After its alliance with Hitler, Japan started building an empire in Southeast Asia. To extend their power in the Pacific, Japan's generals believed they needed to cripple the US navy, based at Pearl Harbor in Hawaii. On December 7, 1941, they launched a surprise attack on the naval base. The United States now had no choice but to join the fight against Japan, Germany, and their allies. The war lasted until 1945, and millions of soldiers died.

A Race War

German and Japanese troops believed that they were superior to people of other races, leading to brutal treatment of those they thought of as inferior. In the greatest crime of all, about 6 million Jews were murdered in the Holocaust, a deliberate attempt to wipe out an entire people.

Understanding PRIMARY SOURCES

The eyewitness accounts in this book are primary sources. A primary source provides direct information about a subject. Examples of primary sources include diaries and letters. Along with the eyewitness accounts in the book, we will also look at some other primary sources, such as photos and drawings, which provide important information about war and the experience of war.

Franklin D. Roosevelt (left) and Winston Churchill (right) were the respective leaders of the United States and Great Britain at the time of World War II.

UNITED KINGDOM
DENMARK
EAST PRUSSIA (GERMANY)
RUSSIA
NETHERLANDS
BELGIUM
GERMANY
POLAND
LUXEMBOURG
FRANCE
CZECHOSLOVAKIA
SWITZERLAND
HUNGARY
ITALY
ROMANIA
YUGOSLAVIA

Germany is shown in purple on this map of Europe at the start of World War II.

The Path to War

In many ways, the peace treaties agreed after World War I made another war inevitable. Germany had agreed to end the fighting without being invaded, and many Germans believed their generals had betrayed them. Adolf Hitler, a corporal in the German army who had been injured in the war, was one supporter of this theory, blaming traitors and Jews for Germany's downfall.

Not Forgotten

One big grievance for many Germans was the way Germany had been treated after the war. The country had lost land to France, Poland, and Czechoslovakia. Germany's armed forces had been dismantled and the country had been forced to hand over vast amounts of money to the victors.

Taking Advantage

After 1929, the world was hit by economic turmoil in what became known as the Great Depression. Germans suffered more than most and they looked for people to blame for their troubles. Foreigners and Jews were presented as the cause of their problems. Adolf Hitler's National Socialist, or Nazi, Party encouraged this view and won 37 percent of votes at an election in 1932. In January 1933, Hitler became Chancellor of Germany.

Europe Goes to War

During the 1930s, Hitler rearmed Germany, while restricting the freedoms of Germans. His supporters attacked or arrested anyone who disagreed with them. In 1938, Hitler invaded German-speaking Austria, where he had been born. Britain and France were desperate to avoid war and allowed him to invade Czechoslovakia. Hitler believed he could do whatever he wanted, but when he attacked Poland on September 1, 1939, Britain and France decided enough was enough, and Europe was once again at war.

WITNESS TO WAR

Paul Schmidt was a translator in the German Foreign Ministry and was with Hitler and his circle of advisors when war was declared. This is an extract from his account:

"*Goering* turned to me and said: 'if we lose this war, then God have mercy on us!' *Goebbels* stood in a corner, downcast and self-absorbed. Everywhere in the room I saw looks of grave concern..."

Goering was an important Nazi military leader.

Goebbels was responsible for the **propaganda** of the Nazis.

What do you think Goering's words tell us about possible concerns among the Germans about what might happen if they did not win the war?

Why do you think Goebbels is described as looking "downcast"?

When German troops invaded Poland by crossing the Vistula River, they had to erect a bridge. The original bridge had been destroyed.

CHAPTER 2

A WORLDWIDE WAR

World War II was fought over a wider area than any previous war. The fighting spread from the rain forests of Southeast Asia to the icy waters of the Arctic Ocean. Troops on all sides were forced to fight far from their homes and would have worried about the safety of the families they left behind, facing bombing raids and other attacks.

War Across the World

The two main theaters of war were Europe and Asia, although there was also significant fighting in North Africa and across the world's oceans. By 1945, the United States military alone numbered more than 12 million men and women. Other countries also fielded vast armies.

A High-Tech War

World War I had been fought mainly by armies of **infantry**, with airplanes and tanks becoming more important later in the war. By the time of World War II, these weapons had become

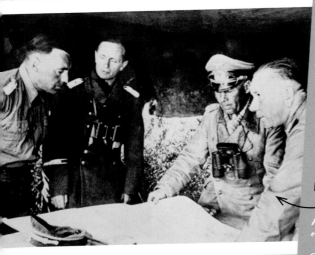

The Desert Fox

This photograph shows the German Field Marshal Erwin Rommel (second from right) discussing the war in Africa with his staff. He was on the Libyan Front at the time, in July 1942. Rommel was a skilled military planner who became famous for his campaigns in North Africa. State-of-the-art German tanks known as "panzers" were used in some of Rommel's campaigns.

Rommel became known as "The Desert Fox" because of his smart battle tactics in the North African desert.

Later in the war, US airplanes carried vital supplies to troops in North Africa.

essential. Tank divisions supported by airplanes and infantry were able to move much more quickly, invading countries in just a few days. At sea, the use of aircraft carriers meant that sea battles could be fought between fleets that could not even see each other.

Ordinary People Go to War

Most of those who fought in World War II were not professional soldiers but ordinary men and women. They fought for their countries far from home, and the safety of their families. The war also devastated the lives of millions of men, women, and children who were not in uniform. Ordinary families were targeted with bombs or attacked by invading forces.

Not only were the battles of World War II fought on land and in the air, they were also fought in oceans and seas.

The Fight in Europe

The first few months of the war in Europe were called the "Phony War." Leaders in Britain had expected bombing raids on its cities to begin the moment war was declared, but this did not happen. However, not long into 1940, Hitler's forces controlled most of Europe. Defeat for the Nazis seemed a very long way away as the people of Britain feared for their future.

Poland Under Attack

Poland was defeated by the Nazis a few weeks after the outbreak of war, with Germany taking the western part and the Soviet Union seizing the east after a pact with Hitler. Poland suffered terribly under Nazi rule, with the murder of around 6 million men, women, and children, including 3 million Jews.

A Lightning Strike

In the west, Britain and France could do little to help Poland. They did not want to attack Germany and suffer heavy losses. Instead they waited for Hitler to make the next move. Then, in April 1940, Germany invaded Denmark and then Norway, followed soon by the Netherlands, Belgium, and France. The Allies had built fortifications known as the Maginot line along the French-German border, but the line did not cross an area of thick forest. The Allies did not think the Germans would attempt to cross it. However, the Germans simply plowed their tanks and vehicles through the forest to enter France, taking the Allies by surprise. The German "lightning war," or blitzkrieg, using tanks and airplanes, was too much for the Allies. Paris was captured on June 14.

The invading Germans were brutal in their treatment of people they considered "inferior." These Polish women were marched into woodland where they were killed.

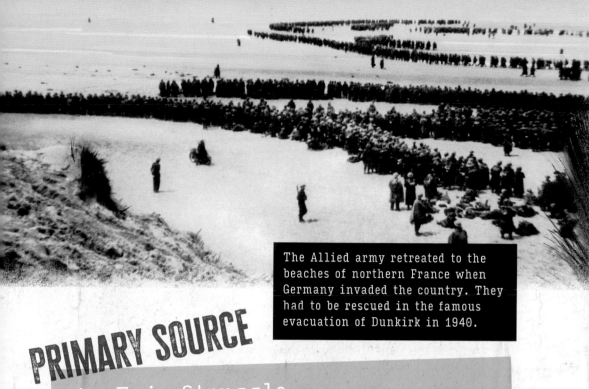

The Allied army retreated to the beaches of northern France when Germany invaded the country. They had to be rescued in the famous evacuation of Dunkirk in 1940.

PRIMARY SOURCE

An Epic Struggle

In 1941, Hitler invaded the vast spaces of the Soviet Union. After early successes, the Nazi advance was stopped in the winter of 1942–43 at the epic Battle of Stalingrad, which claimed the lives of more than 1 million Soviet soldiers. The struggle between Germany and the Soviet Union resulted in brutal fighting, and the loss of around 24 million Soviet citizens. Around 500,000 German soldiers died in the Battle of Stalingrad and about 90,000 German soldiers were taken prisoner by the Soviets.

This photograph shows some of the German soldiers taken captive. What do you think their appearance tells us about the hardships they had endured?

Hitting Back

The Allies retaliated with massive bombing raids on German cities. Around 500,000 Germans died in these raids, compared to about 40,000 British **civilian** deaths in the Blitz. Despite this small victory, the raids were extremely dangerous for the bombers. More than 150,000 Allied aircrew lost their lives.

War at Sea

Before the United States entered the war, ships carried vital weapons and supplies across the Atlantic Ocean to support the Allies. After the attack on Pearl Harbor on December 7, 1941, these ships carried soldiers. German submarines, called U-boats, were a constant menace to the ships in the Battle of the Atlantic. As the war went on, Allied ships and airplanes managed to sink many U-boats through improved technology and by deciphering coded messages.

German bomber airplanes attacked Britain during the war, destroying large parts of cities such as London.

War in the Sky

In World War II, fighter airplanes were used to try to control the skies. The Nazis' plan to invade Britain in 1940 was halted by the pilots of the Royal Air Force (RAF), who destroyed almost twice as many planes of the German Air Force, or Luftwaffe, as they lost themselves in a campaign known as the Battle of Britain.

The Brutal Blitz

When the battle to control the skies was lost, the Luftwaffe changed tactics. Huge fleets of bombers attacked the cities and factories of Britain, killing men, women, and children alike, in what became known as the Blitz.

The surprising and devastating attack by Japanese airplanes on the US naval base in Pearl Harbor, Hawaii, prompted the United States to enter the war.

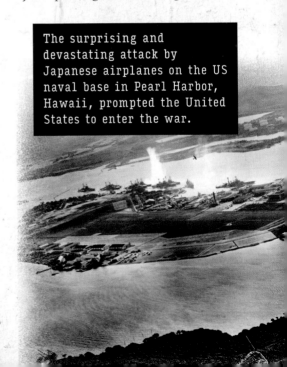

WITNESS TO WAR

British Air Marshal Arthur "Bomber" Harris wrote about the intended result of the bombing of Germany. This is an extract from his accounts:

"The aim of the [Allies'] Combined Bomber Offensive ... should be unambiguously stated [as] the destruction of German cities, the killing of German workers, and the disruption of civilized life throughout Germany."

What can we learn about the Allied attitude to the Germans from these words?

Civilized life includes education, homes, work and workplaces, and leisure activities.

Why would the Allies want to disrupt civilized life throughout Germany? What effect would this likely have on the Germans? What might the Allies gain by doing so?

Shock Attack

The *Honolulu Star-Bulletin* announced the attack on Pearl Harbor on its cover, with the huge headline "War!"

The appearance and tone of the newspaper reporting emphasizes how shocking and significant the attack was for the American people.

Honolulu Star-Bulletin 1st EXTRA

HONOLULU, TERRITORY OF HAWAII, U. S. A., SUNDAY, DECEMBER 7, 1941 — PRICE FIVE CENTS

WAR!

(Associated Press by Transpacific Telephone)

SAN FRANCISCO, Dec. 7.—President Roosevelt announced this morning that Japanese planes had attacked Manila and Pearl Harbor.

OAHU BOMBED BY JAPANESE PLANES

SIX KNOWN DEAD, 21 INJURED, AT EMERGENCY HOSPITAL

Attack Made On Island's

Hundreds See City Bombed

The Fight in the East

The war in Asia and the Pacific was very different from the struggle in Europe. After the attack on Pearl Harbor, Japanese forces seized many territories in the Pacific and Southeast Asia, culminating with the capture of Singapore from the British.

Fighting in Burma

In the rain forests of Burma, British and Indian forces fought a long and difficult battle against the Japanese, who were also waging a fierce campaign with US forces in the Pacific Ocean. Unfortunately for Japan, its attack on Pearl Harbor had failed to destroy US aircraft carriers. These now became central to the campaign, such as at the Battle of Midway, when four Japanese aircraft carriers were destroyed.

Fight to the Death

Both sides knew that Japan's resistance could not last, but the Japanese

US troops fought on island after island in the Pacific to push back the Japanese.

people believed that surrender was dishonorable. In battle after battle on heavily defended Pacific islands such as Saipan and Iwo Jima, US forces attacked Japanese troops who fought to the death. On Saipan, almost all 30,000 Japanese troops were killed, while Japanese women and children jumped off cliffs to avoid capture.

Battle for the Philippines

Japan wanted to build an empire in Asia and formed an alliance with Hitler to help them. After Pearl Harbor, Japan attacked the Philippines and in 1942, US troops were forced to leave the country. But two years later, in a naval battle, Allied forces freed the Philippines again.

It must have been devastating for US troops to leave the Philippines so soon after Pearl Harbor, but Allied forces were determined to resist the occupation of the Japanese.

Never Give In

By the end of 1944, the Japanese were massively outnumbered by US forces. However, Japan's fanatical resistance continued. **Kamikaze pilots** faced certain death as they crashed their planes filled with explosives into US ships. Japanese cities were ruined by US bombing raids, but Japanese families showed a similar determination to fight to the end.

Kamikaze attacks on US ships were devastating, resulting in huge loss of life in many instances.

WITNESS TO WAR

James J. Fahey was a member of the US navy during World War II. He was aboard a US battleship stationed near the Philippines in November 1944 when the ship was attacked by Japanese aircraft. This is an extract from his account of the event:

"Jap planes and bombs were hitting all around us. Some of our ships were being hit by suicide planes, bombs, and machine gun fire. It was a fight to the finish."

What do you think it must have been like for US servicemen aboard the ship while such a savage attack took place?

What do you think is meant by "a fight to the finish"?

CHAPTER 3

FAMILIES ON THE FRONT LINE

During World War II, families were on the front line as never before. For the first time, the numbers of civilian casualties during a war were much greater than the numbers killed on the battlefield. This was partly because the war raged over such a large area, but also because armies on all sides deliberately targeted civilians with their bombing campaigns. The major exception to this was the mainland United States, which was beyond the reach of enemy attack.

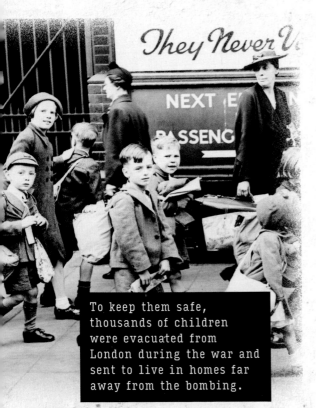

To keep them safe, thousands of children were evacuated from London during the war and sent to live in homes far away from the bombing.

Frightened Families

In almost every country in Europe, apart from **neutral** countries such as Sweden, Switzerland, and Ireland, millions of people were caught up in the fighting itself or had to live under German occupation. Others, including the Germans themselves, faced extreme shortages of food and the prospect of air attack.

Preparing for Attack

At the end of August 1939, Britain passed laws to protect the public, including giving the government the power to **evacuate** people and animals to safe places. Schools were closed in London as children were evacuated to the countryside.

Brutality in Asia

In Asia, Japanese rule was just as brutal as German rule in Europe. In Hong Kong, wounded British soldiers were murdered in their hospital beds. Ordinary people were at constant risk of arrest or execution. Many were forced to work on Japanese war projects, such as building railroads, or confined in labor camps with little food.

Soldiers captured by Japanese troops were kept in camps and starved. Those who did survive their imprisonment were extremely thin by the end of the war.

PRIMARY SOURCE

Japanese Americans Under Guard

Although US civilians did not face the same attacks as others, about 120,000 US citizens were imprisoned during the war. They were Japanese Americans, who lived mostly on the West Coast. There were fears that they would be loyal to Japan in the event of an invasion, so President Roosevelt ordered that all Japanese Americans should be kept in internment camps far from the coast. Many of those who were interned and guarded by soldiers had been born in the United States and had never even visited Japan. This photograph shows a Japanese American family ordered to leave their home in the United States. What impact do you think internment would have had on these families and their lives? Do you think a similar scenario could ever take place today?

Under German Rule

By the summer of 1941, Hitler controlled much of Europe. Some areas, such as western Poland, became part of Germany. German armies occupied Denmark, Norway, Belgium, the Netherlands, and most of France. Southern France and many parts of Eastern Europe had their own governments, but they followed Hitler's orders—some willingly, others not. In 1941, the prospect of liberation by the Allies was a very distant one.

Lost Freedoms

Just like people in Nazi Germany, the people living under occupation faced many restrictions on their lives. They were not free to express their opinions, as any criticism of the invading Nazis would be harshly punished. The Nazis also controlled all forms of communication about the war, such as newspapers and the radio. Nazi rule was brutally enforced by the **SS** (Schutzstaffel—German for Protection Squadron), led by Heinrich Himmler. German rule was harshest in Eastern Europe, especially Poland. After the war, the Nazis planned to settle Germans in the lands they controlled.

Forced to Work

The conquered countries were looted to support the German war effort. Food and raw materials were taken away. Many people were forced to work for the Nazi war machine, such as in building military fortifications. Others were taken to Germany to work.

Heinrich Himmler (left) and Heydrich Reinhard (right) were two of the most senior Nazis that helped Hitler carry out his brutal plans.

Courage Under Fire

Under this cruel regime, it took huge courage to join the resistance to Nazi rule, but many people did. Men and women, often helped by Allied secret agents, **sabotaged** Nazi vehicles and communications. Resistance fighters also helped hide escaped prisoners and Jews fleeing the Nazis. Resistance attacks on German officials were punished with massacres of innocent people.

In France, both women and men took up arms to fight the Germans and resist their onslaught.

Murdered for Fighting Back

On June 10, 1944, 643 men, women, and children from the village of Oradour-sur-Glane in western France were murdered in retaliation for resistance activities. The village itself was partly burned to the ground.

Although there are no survivors to tell the story of this village, the ruins shown in this photograph have been preserved as a memorial to the victims of the Nazi occupation.

Britain Is Bombed

When Germany became involved in the Spanish Civil War (1936–1939), their bombing of the Spanish town of Guernica in 1937 showed the catastrophic damage that could be done to civilians and their homes by vast fleets of bombers. In September 1940, when Hitler was forced to cancel his invasion of Britain, he ordered that the people of Britain's cities should be bombed into submission.

Taking Shelter

Britain had been preparing for air attacks. Public shelters were built, and many Londoners spent the night in subway stations. Air raid wardens patrolled the streets at night to make sure that cities were in complete darkness, to make it difficult for bombers to find their targets. Many teenagers were among those who volunteered to keep watch for fires.

PRIMARY SOURCE

Attacks on London and Coventry

The Blitz on London began on September 7, 1940. For the next six months, thousands of bombs were dropped on the city every month. As well as London and its docks, the bombers targeted coastal ports and other industrial cities. In November, many tons of explosives and 900 incendiary bombs (designed to start fires) were dropped on the city of Coventry in a single night. This photograph shows firefighters in an area of London that has been hit by German aircraft. What effect do you think the Blitz had on firefighters who had to repeatedly tackle the blazes?

Unbreakable Spirit

There was less bombing after May 1941, but the menace did not stop completely. Later in the war, Britain's families were terrorized by V1 and V2 flying bombs that could destroy a whole street of houses. The Blitz was designed to destroy the **morale** of the British people. Instead, it encouraged a strong determination and community spirit that helped the country through the darkest days of the war. There was also a strong thirst for revenge on Germany and support for the terrible bombing raids carried out against German cities by Allied airplanes.

Words from Winston

This speech by Prime Minister Winston Churchill was broadcast on February 9, 1941.

"[Hitler] sought to break the spirit of the British nation by the bombing, first of London, and afterward of our great cities. It has now been proved ... that this form of blackmail by murder and terrorism, so far from weakening the spirit of the British nation, has only roused it to a more intense and universal flame than was ever seen before in any modern community."

Winston Churchill visited the ruins of Coventry Cathedral in 1941. Coventry was one of the British cities devastated by German bombing during the Blitz.

A Lost Childhood

The war altered societies so much that every family member saw parts of their life change. In Britain, many children in the cities were evacuated to live with families in the country for the duration of the war. In other countries, children survived as well as they could. The young were not spared the worst crimes of the Nazi regime.

A War of Separation

Millions of children in all the warring countries faced long periods of separation from their fathers and other family members, who were serving in the military overseas. At the end of the war, many young children could not even remember what their fathers looked like. Young Americans helped the war effort by raising money and collecting supplies for troops serving in Europe and the Pacific. The government called on families to collect scrap metal to make into weapons for the war.

PRIMARY SOURCE

Happy and Sad

These children were evacuated to the countryside. They are photographed carrying their gas masks. Three million children from Britain's cities were sent to live in the country at the start of the war. For some, this experience of country life was a happy one, in spite of the dangers and problems of wartime. They had escaped the city and saw real fields and farm animals for the first time. For others, evacuation was a very unpleasant experience, living with strangers and missing their families. What do you think parents must have felt about having to send their children away to live with strangers?

In Warsaw, Poland, thousands of Jewish families were rounded up by German soldiers and sent to camps. Most did not survive.

All Victims

Many children lost their homes and families during the war or were targeted themselves. Hundreds of thousands of Jewish children were murdered by the Nazis. Some Jewish children were lucky enough to be evacuated from Germany and elsewhere in Europe before the war in a rescue operation called the Kindertransport. Their own lives were saved, but many never saw their families or homes again.

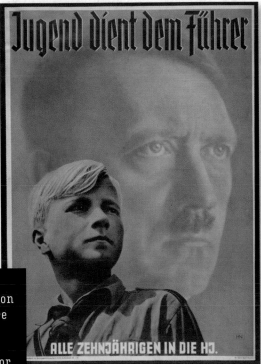

Jugend dient dem Führer

ALLE ZEHNJÄHRIGEN IN DIE HJ.

In Germany, children were encouraged to join an organization called "Hitler Youth." They were trained to support their leader, Adolf Hitler, the war, and the idea that Germans were a superior race. This poster reads "Youth serves the leader—all ten-year-olds into the Hitler Youth."

CHAPTER 4

WOMEN AND THE WAR

Women's lives changed in many ways during the war. In the warring countries, normal family life continued, but with the added danger of air raids, or the inconvenience of dealing with wartime rules and shortages. However, for many women, particularly in the Allied nations such as the United States and Great Britain, war was a time of opportunity. They could take on new jobs and support the military effort in other ways.

In Canada and the United States, women worked in munitions factories to ensure that troops overseas had the weaponry they needed to fight the war.

An Allied Advantage

Family life was very hard for many families. With fathers, brothers, and sons serving overseas, the full burden of working and bringing up children fell on women. In the Allied countries, many women also went out to work. The Nazis had a very traditional view that most women should stay at home in their roles as wives and mothers. The more effective use of women as part of the war effort was a big advantage for the Allies.

Women in the Resistance

Millions of women had to manage family life under German occupation. Just as in the male population, some women chose to **collaborate** with the invaders, or stay out of trouble. But others were actively involved in the resistance—hiding **fugitives**, passing messages, or helping with sabotage missions. Genevieve Soulié was a member of the French Resistance who helped more than 100 Allied airmen escape capture by the Nazis.

Women Protestors

Women were less likely to be suspected than men but, if caught, they faced imprisonment or execution. German student Sophie Scholl was a member of the White Rose, a peaceful resistance movement. Scholl and her fellow members opposed the Nazis, producing leaflets criticizing Hitler and his supporters. In 1943, Scholl was executed after her opposition was discovered.

Women not only worked on ammunition and weapons, they also welded metal to help create vehicles such as airplanes.

WITNESS TO WAR

Else Gebel was Sophie's cellmate in her last days. Below is an extract from her account of some of Sophie's last conversations with her:

Sophie was just 21 years old when she died.

" ... how many have to die on the battlefield in these days, how many young promising lives. What does my death matter if by our acts thousands are warned and alerted."

What do you think Sophie meant by asking this question?

Who do you think she was hoping to warn and alert?

Do you think young people today would be prepared to make a similar sacrifice if faced with her circumstances?

Women of all ages were involved in the war effort. Many had sons who were fighting overseas, and wanted to support them by working in factories at home.

Women and the War Effort

By the end of the war, 1 in 4 married women in the United States were working, and 37 percent of the country's workers were women. In Britain, over 7 million women were employed in war work by 1944. All women had to register for war work, and unmarried women had a choice between working or joining the military in supporting roles.

Women in the Factories

During the war, almost 7 million women joined the workforce in the United States. These workers often had husbands serving in the military. Many of the jobs they took on involved hard, physical work that had previously been done by men. Women worked cutting steel, welding, and riveting tanks and airplanes. More than half of those working in the aviation industry were women. The image of Rosie the Riveter, the US government's idea of a **patriotic** female worker, became a successful campaign for recruiting more workers.

Working on the Land

As well as working in factories, women were also needed to work on the land. In Britain, it became very difficult to import food, so most things had to be grown at home.

Young women could be conscripted, or forced, to take on essential war jobs. By 1943, more than 80,000 women had joined the Women's Land Army (WLA). The Women's Land Army of America (WLAA) dealt with a shortage of labor on farms in the US. What do you think it must have been like to have been forced to work on a farm without any prior experience?

PRIMARY SOURCE

Not an Equal War

Many women war workers earned more than they had before the war. A waitress could now earn much more in a munitions factory, but the work was difficult and could be dangerous. This female worker (below) is checking bomb cases loaded with explosives in a factory in Nebraska. The US National War Labor Board (NWLB) tried to ensure equal pay for men and women doing the same job, but employers often skirted the rules. On average, women earned $6 compared to $10 for a man doing a similar job. Labor unions were most concerned about working men, so did not fight hard for more rights for women. Do you think a similar scenario would happen today? Why or why not?

Women on the Front Line

During World War II, women were closer to the front line than ever before, although only in the Soviet Union were women allowed to fight in the war. However, in many other countries women joined the military services. They provided support to frontline forces both at home and abroad.

As the war continued, some women joined civil defense units and were ready to fight if the United States was invaded.

WITNESS TO WAR

Meda Brendall worked seven days a week as a shipyard welder in Baltimore, Maryland. She took her work seriously, believing that she was doing her part to help the war effort. Here are extracts from a series of interviews with her:

"I understood in any job ... you have to use your own discipline ... I wasn't there to fool around, I was there for the war effort, and I was there to weld for our boys overseas ... It's a good thing that the women went in ... it's a good thing that they showed the world what they could do."

The war effort was any activity that supported the fight against the enemy.

What do you think Meda meant by women showing the world what they could do?

How do you think attitudes toward women may have changed because of their contribution to the war effort?

Behind the Troops

Women had first been organized in support roles for the military forces in World War I. Many of these groups were revived when World War II broke out. In Britain, young women could be conscripted into the Auxiliary Territorial Service (ATS) or the Women's Royal Naval Service (WRNS). As well as supporting the troops with roles such as cooking and administration, women also operated vehicles and antiaircraft guns.

Fighting and Spying

Around 800,000 Soviet women actually fought on the front line, in airplanes and tanks, and as snipers. Elsewhere, women took on duties that put them in grave danger, such as medical roles with frontline soldiers, or on warships. Some women were trained as spies and worked behind enemy lines.

PRIMARY SOURCE

Joining Up

In the United States, more than 350,000 women joined branches of the armed forces such as the Women's Army Corps (WAC) and the US navy's Women Accepted for Volunteer Emergency Service (WAVES). More than 1,000 women were members of the Women Airforce Service Pilots (WASP) program, flying planes in noncombat roles, such as delivering airplanes to bases and carrying cargo. This photograph shows a group of WASP pilots. Nearly 40 female pilots died on missions. How do you think that the efforts and sacrifices of women fighters may have changed attitudes toward women in the armed forces?

160449A.C

CHAPTER 5

FUNDING THE WAR

Factories, shipyards, and other parts of the economy worked around the clock producing the materials that were needed, so that when a ship was sunk or an airplane shot down, many more would be ready to take its place. The people of the warring countries were asked to make sacrifices, because basic materials and foods were in short supply. Free speech was also restricted as governments sought to raise morale at home and abroad.

Building Better

In their attempts to win the war, both sides used every resource they could. Even before the United States entered the war, its factories and shipyards produced ships and other supplies for the Allies. Liberty Ships were specially designed ships that could be built quickly for the war. They were manufactured in sections and welded together for use as transportation ships. A workforce of 650,000, more than 10 percent of whom were women, built 2,700 of these ships, of which about 200 were lost during the war.

Almost 3,000 Liberty Ships were built during the war to carry vital supplies to Allied troops.

No Match for the United States

Once the United States began to send millions of troops overseas, all the country's industry was dedicated to the war effort. President Roosevelt set the nation a target of producing 50,000 airplanes in a year. By 1944, the country was producing more than 90,000. The wartime economies of Germany and Japan could never hope to match this industrial might.

Paying for the War

Producing armaments and supplying the armed forces cost many billions of dollars. To fund the war, the United States issued **war bonds**, which individuals could buy. Official campaigns tried to convince Americans that buying war bonds was their patriotic duty. Germany used the economies of the countries it invaded to fund its wartime economy, along with forced labor.

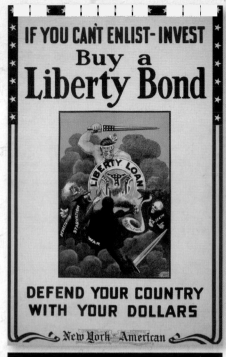

IF YOU CAN'T ENLIST - INVEST
Buy a Liberty Bond

LIBERTY LOAN

DEFEND YOUR COUNTRY WITH YOUR DOLLARS

New York American

Liberty bonds were war bonds that Americans could buy. The money they spent on them went toward paying for weapons, ammunitions, and other supplies for soldiers.

Benefits of the War

As well as women, the World War II brought many Black people into the workforce as demand for workers soared. Wages rose and conditions for many people were better than they had been during the years of depression in the 1930s.

Black people played an active role both on the front line and at home. This photograph shows Black workers shaking and stacking peanuts in Georgia in 1943. They had volunteered to harvest peanuts that could be used to create oil to help the war effort.

The Problem of Food

Coping with shortages became a way of life for many people. Much of Europe's food was imported from overseas. The merchant ships that carried food were under threat from submarine attack, so this trade was badly affected. Goods like steel and gasoline were in demand for making and powering ships, tanks, and airplanes, so people were urged to use less and avoid waste. Shortages even affected neutral countries such as Sweden.

Enough for All

In Britain, the Ministry of Food was set up to make sure that everyone had enough to eat. Each person was issued with a **ration** book, allowing only a small amount of certain foods every week. A poster campaign urged people to "Dig for Victory" and grow their own food, so every available piece of land was used to grow vegetables. Shortages even continued after the war, and candy was rationed until 1953.

PRIMARY SOURCE

Do Not Waste

Americans were urged to do without luxuries and cut waste to help the war effort. Factories were altered so they could make goods for the war, supplying troops overseas and the United States' allies. Although shortages were not as severe as in Britain, many foods were rationed to make sure that people did not hoard food. Communities held scrap and salvage drives to collect and recycle metal and other useful goods. The image below shows ration books used in the United States. What do you think it may have been like to have lived during a time of rations? Do you think people today would accept similar restrictions?

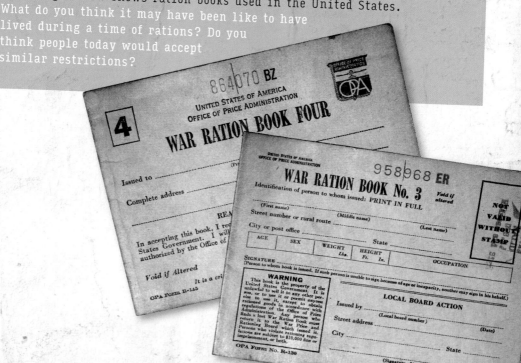

Starving Them Out

During World War I, thousands of people in Germany had starved due to food shortages. Hitler knew the risks of lack of food, and so rationing was introduced in Germany before the war even started. Food from the countries the Nazis invaded was used to feed Germans, while many people across Europe had very little to eat. In Nazi-controlled Europe, even rationing was decided on racial grounds. Jews were given the least, followed by Poles and Czechs. The Nazis deliberately planned to let millions of people in Eastern Europe starve. Rations were cut dramatically in the later stages of the war, even for Germans.

This American woman is reading a government brochure that explains why rationing is required to help win the war.

Areas of public land, such as Boston Common, were plowed during the war to create areas in which important food crops could be grown.

The Information War

All governments during wartime used information and propaganda to control and build the morale of their own citizens, and to attack their enemies. Propaganda is information that is produced to achieve a political goal. Sometimes, this is obvious, such as in the posters on this page. At other times, the fact that something is propaganda can be less clear.

A War of Words

In Germany, the Nazis controlled all branches of media and the arts, strictly limiting what people could say or write. They also produced propaganda directed against the Allies, and particularly against those people they believed were the enemies of Germany, such as Jews, Poles, and Russians. This action was led by Joseph Goebbels, who oversaw the Reich Ministry of Public Enlightenment and Propaganda.

Information Is Power

In 1942, President Roosevelt created the Office of War Information to help rally American support for the war effort. Posters, cartoons, and other media presented the United States' enemies as monsters that must be defeated. Americans were urged to work hard for victory. Similar methods were used in Britain, where newspapers and radio broadcasts were **censored** so that the news from the war was always positive.

So wie wir kämpfen

Helfe Du für den Sieg!

Both the Germans and the Allies created war propaganda, like the posters shown here. The poster above says "As We Fight—Work for Victory!" The information was designed to encourage people to continue to support the war.

LET'S CATCH HIM WITH HIS "PANZERS" DOWN!

WE WILL- IF WE KEEP 'EM FIRING!

Radio and Movies

Roosevelt, Churchill, and other leaders used radio to communicate with their people. Movies were also used to inspire citizens. Director Frank Capra created a series of documentary movies called *Why We Fight*. In Britain, Laurence Olivier's movie of Shakespeare's *Henry V* rallied people with past victories. Cartoons were used to persuade people that the war was justified—in one, Donald Duck attacked Hitler with a tomato!

Words Winning the War

When the tide of war turned against Germany, Goebbels knew that Allied propaganda leaflets dropped from airplanes, and radio broadcasts from Britain, were having a great impact on the people of Germany and damaging their morale.

These Allied soldiers are filling shells with propaganda leaflets. The leaflets were then dropped into Germany and occupied countries.

PRIMARY SOURCE

UNITED we are strong

UNITED we will win

Keep Strong

This poster was created in the United States in 1943. The flags of Allied countries are shown on the cannons. What do you think people may have felt when they viewed this poster?

CHAPTER 6

WIPING OUT PEOPLE

Many more civilians died in World War II than fighters killed on the battlefield. The worst crimes were inflicted on ordinary families who were simply trying to live their lives in peace. The Allies were not blameless —half a million Germans died in British and American bombing raids. Worst of all was the fate of Europe's Jews, whom the Nazis tried to wipe out completely.

People Persecuted

Almost as soon as they took power, the Nazis started to create **concentration camps** to imprison **communists** and other political enemies. The Nazis believed that the German race was superior to others, and that this gave them the right to **persecute** those they thought were inferior, including Russians, Poles, and disabled people. Racial violence was not restricted to the Nazis. In Croatia, an ally of Germany, Serbs were massacred by the authorities. The Japanese also persecuted civilians in the countries they invaded, especially in China.

Jews and other people that the Nazis considered inferior were subjected to horrific treatment in camps that they were sent to during the war.

Race Crime

This image shows a Russian man who was held in a concentration camp by the Nazis during the war. The photograph was taken in 1945, when he was freed from the camp. The Russian is identifying a Nazi who was one of the officers at the camp. How do you think both the Russian prisoner and the Nazi officer felt at the point this photograph was taken?

A Prisoner's Fate

The rights of prisoners of war to receive humane treatment were supposed to be guaranteed by an agreement called the **Geneva Convention**. Tens of thousands of men and women were captured and held as prisoners between 1939 and 1945, but their treatment varied considerably. British and US soldiers in German camps were usually treated according to the rules, as were prisoners in British and US camps. Prisoners on the **Eastern Front** were treated brutally by both sides, often starved, and forced into slave labor. Many Germans captured by the Russians never returned home.

Japan did not recognize the Geneva Convention, and Allied prisoners in Asia often faced terrible conditions.

Murder of the Jews

The Nazis' hatred of the Jews had been clear from the start. During the 1930s, the Nazis had stripped Jews in Germany of their rights and property. Life for Jewish people had been made unbearable, forcing many to leave their homes and settle overseas. The conquest of Poland and other parts of Eastern Europe brought many more Jews under Nazi control. In late 1941, Germany began the systematic, organized murder of millions of Jews, which is known as the Holocaust.

A Jewish Horror

Hitler had already decreed that Jewish prisoners should be executed during the invasion of Russia. Many Jews had been crammed into **ghettos** where they died from hunger and disease. One of the largest ghettos was in Warsaw, Poland.

Worked to Death or Poisoned

From the beginning of 1942, the Nazis began to transport Jews from across Europe to death camps in Poland. Those who were strong enough would work until they were too weak to work any more. Others would be murdered, often using poison gas.

The scale of this crime was so great that when people who managed to escape the clutches of the Nazis revealed the truth to the outside world, few people believed them.

A Terrible Truth

The awful truth became clear as Allied soldiers regained territory from Germany in the later months of the war. The SS guards moved prisoners around on forced marches to keep them, and the evidence of the Nazis' crimes, from being released by the Allies. Of Europe's 9 million Jews at the start of the war, around 6 million were murdered in the Holocaust.

These Hungarian Jews were sent to one of the most famous German death camps, Auschwitz, in Poland, in 1944.

When people in the German death camps were finally liberated, or freed, the true horror of the Nazis and their treatment of the Jews came to light.

WITNESS TO WAR

In the years following the war, Holocaust survivors testified about their experiences so their captors could be brought to justice. This is the testimony of one survivor, Dora Almaleh.

"One day in April 1945 whilst at Belsen I was working in the vegetable store when I saw a Hungarian girl, whose name I do not know, come out of the bread store nearby carrying a loaf of bread. At this moment [Karl] Egersdorf appeared in the street and at a distance of about 6 meters from the girl shouted, 'What are you doing here?' The girl replied, 'I am hungry' and then started to run away. Egersdorf immediately pulled out his pistol and shot the girl."

Belsen was a large concentration camp in Germany.

Why do you think Egersdorf killed the girl with seemingly so little thought, and what does that tell you about how the lives of the captives at Belsen were viewed by German soldiers?

CHAPTER 7

THE WAR COMES TO AN END

After the successful landing of Allied forces on the beaches of Normandy in June 1944, it became clear that the Allies would eventually win the war. Hitler's advance into Russia had been stopped in the apocalyptic Battle of Stalingrad. Since then, Nazi armies in the east had been in retreat. Millions of US soldiers tipped the balance in the west. Elsewhere, Japan fought a desperate struggle for survival.

The End in Europe

Germany was being squeezed between the armies of the Soviet Union on one side, and the Allied forces of the United States, Britain, Canada, and others in the west.

Hitler declared that there would be no surrender, so the war dragged on until the Soviet Red Army captured Berlin, and Hitler, in his underground bunker, shot himself. Families around the world celebrated Victory in Europe Day on May 8, 1945.

PRIMARY SOURCE

Rising Up

This photograph shows a French man and woman fighting with weapons they had taken from the Germans in Paris in August 1944. Once the Allies defeated the Germans in Normandy, people in Paris revolted against the Germans. Why do you think the events in Normandy encouraged them that it was time to act?

Race for the Bomb

Japan refused to be beaten until two of its cities were destroyed by a weapon so powerful that even Japan's fanatical leaders had to admit defeat. Both sides in the war had been trying to develop an **atomic bomb**. The United States won the race, partly due to Jewish scientists who had fled the Nazis. The first atomic bomb was dropped on the city of Hiroshima, Japan, on August 6, 1945, and it killed as many as 80,000 men, women, and children in seconds. Three days later another bomb was dropped, on the city of Nagasaki. On August 15, 1945, the Emperor of Japan surrendered—and the war was over at last.

The dropping of atomic bombs on Japan finally ended the war, but with enormous and horrific cost.

WITNESS TO WAR

This is an extract from a diary written by a survivor of the bombing of Hiroshima. His name was Dr Michihiko Hachiya.

"There were the shadowy forms of people, some of whom looked like walking ghosts. Others moved as though in pain, like scarecrows, their arms held out from their bodies with forearms and hands dangling ... I suddenly realized that they had been burned ..."

What effect do you think the realization that so many people had been badly burned would have had on Dr Hachiya and other eyewitnesses? Do you think the bombing of Japan to end the war was justifiable?

The Legacy of War

At the end of the war, much of Europe was in ruins, and so was Japan. No one knows quite how many people died in the war, but some estimates put the figure at 60 million people, more than half of whom were civilians. Millions of people were left homeless because of bombing or because they had been released from camps. **Refugees** rushed to escape from Eastern Europe as communist governments were set up by the Soviet Union. German families in particular were forced to leave homes in the East, where many had lived for generations.

It would take an enormous effort for the warring countries, and the families shattered by war, to rebuild their lives after the war ended in 1945.

Children of the War

The children of World War II grew up in a very different world. The victors did not stay united for long, and the United States and the Soviet Union, the two "superpowers" to emerge from the war, soon faced each other in a tense standoff known as the Cold War. The experiences of families varied greatly, depending on where in the world they lived.

Memorials such as this one showing US marines raising the American flag in Iwo Jima, in the Pacific, remind people of the great sacrifice that troops made during the war.

Winners and Losers

The United States was more powerful than ever in 1945. Her industries and military might had been strengthened by the war, while former rivals such as Germany and Great Britain had been weakened by defeat or the huge cost of war. Under the Marshall Plan, the United States gave Europe financial aid to help it rebuild, but the road to recovery would be a long one. For families in the United States, 1945 was the beginning of an era of prosperity after the hardships of war.

These two men are sitting among the ruins of Berlin in 1945. The war had cost Germany dearly and it would take many years before the country's cities and people recovered.

The Rise of a Superpower

Families around the world also lived with the fear of another war as tensions rose between the United States and the Soviet Union, and their allies. In 1945, the United Nations (UN) organization was established to try to prevent future wars. However, there were still conflicts as each side tried to prevent the other from gaining too much influence around the world.

The Story for Germany

It was many decades before the people of Eastern Europe escaped the communist regimes that had been imposed by the Soviet Union after the war. In 1990, Germany, which had been divided into East and West Germany, became one country again—and the most powerful member of the European Union. Today, Germany remains one of Europe's most influential countries.

A TIMELINE FOR WAR

This timeline charts the key events of World War II.

1939	**September 1:** Germany invades Poland. **September 3:** Great Britain and France declare war on Germany.
1940	**April 9:** German troops invade Denmark and Norway. **May 10:** German invasion of France, Belgium, and the Netherlands begins. Winston Churchill becomes British Prime Minister. **June 10:** Italy enters the war, declaring war on Britain and France. **June 22:** France signs an armistice with Germany, leaving Germany in control of most of France apart from some of the south, controlled by the German-friendly Vichy government. **July 10:** The Battle of Britain begins as Germany prepares an invasion force. The invasion plan is abandoned in September after Germany fails to defeat the RAF. **September 27:** Germany, Italy, and Japan sign the Tripartite Pact to form the **Axis Powers**. By the end of 1940, Hungary, Romania, and Slovakia have joined them.
1941	**February:** Germany sends Africa Corps to North Africa to support Italian troops. **June 22:** Operation Barbarossa—the German invasion of Russia—begins. **December 7:** Japan attacks the US naval base at Pearl Harbor and begins invasion of Southeast Asia. The United States declares war on Japan the following day.

1942

May 30: British airplanes launch a major bombing raid on Cologne, the start of the bombing of German cities that would continue until 1945.

June 3: The Battle of Midway between the US and Japanese navies begins.

August: The Battle of Stalingrad begins, in which Soviet troops finally halt the German advance. The battle lasts until February 1943.

1943

April 19: Nazi troops start to put down a Jewish uprising in Warsaw Ghetto, in Poland.

July 5: The beginning of the Battle of Kursk on the Eastern Front, the biggest tank battle in history.

July 10: Allied troops from Africa land on the island of Sicily to begin the invasion of Italy.

September 8: Italian surrender is announced. A month later, Italy declares war on Germany.

1944

June 6: Normandy landings by Allied Forces on beaches of France.

August 25: The liberation of Paris takes place, followed soon after by most of France.

October 20: US troops land in the Philippines to begin liberation.

1945

January 27: The liberation of Auschwitz death camp by Soviet troops takes place.

May 8: VE—Victory in Europe—Day is celebrated.

August 6: The first atomic bomb is dropped on Hiroshima, Japan, followed by Nagasaki atomic bomb three days later.

August 15: VJ—Victory over Japan—Day marks the end of World War II.

GLOSSARY

Allies countries fighting against the Axis Powers in World War II

atomic bomb a bomb that splits apart uranium atoms to create a huge explosion

Axis Powers Germany, Japan, Italy, and their allies during World War II

censored restricted access to information or media

civilian a person who is not in the armed forces

collaborate to work together with an invading force, often against your own people

communists people who believe in creating an equal society through government control of property and many other areas of life

concentration camps prison camps where a government imprisons its enemies

Eastern Front border between the land controlled by Germany and the Soviet Union in World War II, where fighting took place

evacuate to move away from a building or other location

fugitives people who have escaped from captivity or are in hiding

Geneva Convention an agreement about rules to be followed in wartime, including the treatment of prisoners

ghettos areas where a group of people are forced to live, such as Jews living in the Warsaw Ghetto during World War II

infantry soldiers marching or fighting on foot

kamikaze pilots Japanese pilots who carried out suicide attacks during World War II

morale the confidence, enthusiasm, or togetherness of a person or group of people

neutral not favoring one side or the other

patriotic showing strong support for your country

persecute to target, or discriminate against, a particular person or group

propaganda information designed to promote a particular message

ration a restriction on how much food and other items people can buy

refugees people who are forced to leave their home because of war or persecution

sabotaged deliberately attempted to weaken an enemy by destroying technology or other materials, such as transportation links

Soviet Union a group of countries, including Russia, that existed from 1922 until 1991

SS elite soldiers of Nazi Germany who enforced Nazi rule with police and military powers

war bonds ways for ordinary people to lend money to the government as a type of investment, to cover expenses during wartime

FIND OUT MORE

Books

Milner Halls, Kelly. *Heroes of World War II: A World War II Book for Kids* (People and Events in History). Rockridge Press, 2021.

Milner Halls, Kelly. *World War II History for Kids: 500 Facts* (History Facts for Kids). Rockridge Press, 2021.

Owens, Lisa L. *Women Pilots of World War II* (Alternator Books). Lerner Publishing Group, 2023.

Websites

Discover more about the United States in wartime on the website of The National WWII Museum in New Orleans, at:
www.nationalww2museum.org

Explore the United States home front in World War II, at:
www.smithsonianeducation.org/idealabs/wwii

For information on, and tributes to, those who died and suffered in the Holocaust, see the website of the United States Holocaust Memorial Museum, at:
www.ushmm.org

Publisher's note to educators and parents:
All the websites featured above have been carefully reviewed to ensure that they are suitable for students. However, many websites change often, and we cannot guarantee that a site's future contents will continue to meet our high standards of educational value. Please be advised that students should be closely monitored whenever they access the Internet.

INDEX

Africa 5, 8, 9
air and naval power 5, 8, 9, 10, 12, 13, 14, 15, 16, 20, 21, 24, 25, 26, 29, 30, 31, 32, 35, 44, 45
Asia and the Pacific 5, 8, 14, 17, 22, 37, 42
Atlantic, Battle of the 12
atomic bomb 41, 45

Belgium 6, 10, 18
Blitz 12, 20, 21
bombing campaigns 8, 9, 10, 12, 13, 15, 16, 20, 21, 27, 36, 41, 42, 44, 45
Britain 5, 6, 10, 12, 13, 14, 16, 17, 20, 21, 22, 24, 26, 27, 29, 32, 34, 35, 36, 37, 40, 43
Britain, Battle of 12, 20, 44

children 4, 9, 10, 12, 14, 16, 17, 19, 22, 23, 24, 41, 42
Churchill, Winston 5, 21, 35, 44
civilian casualties 9, 10, 12, 16, 20, 36, 42
concentration camps 36–39
Czechoslovakia 6, 33

evacuations 11, 16, 22, 23

farming 22, 27
food shortages 16, 17, 18, 27, 30, 32, 33, 37, 38, 39
France 5, 6, 10, 11, 18, 19, 40, 45

Geneva Convention 37
Germany 4, 5, 6, 7, 8, 10, 11, 12, 13, 16, 17, 18, 19, 20, 21, 23, 24, 25, 31, 33, 34, 35, 36, 37, 38, 39, 40, 42, 43
Great Depression 6, 31

Hitler, Adolf 4, 5, 6, 7, 10, 11, 14, 18, 20, 21, 23, 25, 33, 35, 38, 40
Holocaust 5, 37–39

Italy 5, 6

Japan 5, 12, 14, 15, 17, 31, 36, 37, 40, 41, 42
Jews 5, 6, 10, 19, 23, 33, 34, 36, 37–39, 41

Liberty Ships 30

Midway, Battle of 14, 45
mortality figures 5, 11, 12, 14, 16, 29, 36, 41, 42

Nazis 6, 7, 10, 11, 12, 18, 19, 22, 23, 24, 25, 33, 34, 36, 37, 38, 40, 41
neutral countries 16, 32
Normandy landings 40, 45

Pearl Harbor 5, 12, 13, 14, 44
Poland 5, 6, 7, 10, 18, 23, 33, 34, 36, 37, 38
prisoners of war 11, 17, 19, 23, 36, 37, 38, 39, 42
propaganda 7, 18, 26, 31, 32, 34, 35

resistance movement 18, 19, 24, 25
Roosevelt, Franklin D. 5, 17, 31, 34, 35

Soviet Union 5, 6, 10, 11, 28, 29, 34, 36, 37, 38, 40, 42, 43
Stalingrad, Battle of 11, 40, 45

troops 5, 6, 7, 8, 9, 10, 11, 14, 15, 17, 22, 24, 28, 29, 30, 31, 32, 40, 42, 44, 45

United States 5, 8, 9, 12, 13, 14, 15, 16, 17, 24, 26, 27, 28, 29, 30, 31, 32, 33, 34, 35, 36, 37, 40, 41, 42, 43

women 8, 9, 10, 12, 14, 19, 24–29, 30, 31, 37, 41

About the Author

Kelly Roberts has written many history books for young people. In researching the eyewitness accounts in this book, she has learned more about the human experience of war and the devastation it caused for those who witnessed it.